FREE 40

*Quitting Alcohol in Forty Days
(And Changing Your Relationship with
Alcohol Forever!)*

Aaron Blake

© Copyright, 2023. Aaron Blake

Published and Printed in the United States

First Edition

All Rights Reserved.

No part of this book may be reproduced, distributed, or transmitted in any form or by any means, including, but not limited to, photocopying, recording, or other electronic methods, without the prior written permission of the publisher, except in the case of brief quotations embodied in critical reviews and certain other noncommercial uses permitted by copyright law.

The author and publisher specifically disclaim any liability, loss, or risk that is incurred as a consequence, directly or indirectly, of the use and application of any of the contents of this book.

ISBN : 978-1-917007-21-4

This book is dedicated to my sons Jagger, Maverick and River.

Table of Contents

Prologue i

Introduction iii

Chapter 1: 1
Meet Aaron ....

Chapter 2: 7
The Mission Begins ....

Chapter 3: 10
Why Quarantena (40 Days) ....

Chapter 4 (Ty): 12
Free Forty ....

Chapter 5: 15
The Captain of the Team: Alcohol ....

Chapter 6: 17
The Compromise ....

Chapter 7: 24
Who and Hats ....

Chapter 8: 31
Where ....

Chapter 9: When 33

Chapter 10:	35
What And the ABCs of Free 40	
Chapter 11:	38
Why-The Most Important Feature	
Chapter 12:	50
How	
Chapter 13:	61
Are You Wet Or Dry?	
Chapter 14:	63
Support and Supportive Thinking	
Chapter 15:	65
Let's Chat Indulge Mode	
Chapter 16:	68
A New Way Of Drinking: Indulge Mode	
Chapter 17:	73
PPF-PNN Scale (Past-Present-Future/Positive-Neutral-Negative)	
Chapter 18:	77
More Free 40 Mindset Strategies	
Chapter 19:	82
Finale Aka Cured	
Tracking Sheet Suggestions	84
Stay Connected with Aaron Blake	86
Acknowledgements	
About the Author	

Prologue

"Part of the problem of abstinence is that it leaves problem drinkers who are unwilling to, or unable to, give up booze entirely. Presented with a binary (keep drinking heavily or never have another drink), they chose the former. That may be why only 10% of problem drinkers ever seek help. Given that heavy alcohol use puts people at increased risk for disease and early death, the goal is to get more of the other 90% to seek control of their drinking even if they can't fully quit."

(Time Magazine Special Edition. The Science of Addiction December 2021)

Free 40 is here for the other 90%.

Introduction

Welcome to Free 40! I am glad you are here entertaining the idea of changing your relationship with alcohol. I am sure you have a great reason for reading my book, and I'm glad you are taking the steps to consider a different opportunity. I have been reflecting for over five years about how I could improve myself as an individual, husband, father, worker, community member, and friend; part of the solution was there all along. Drink less. The concept is as hard to execute as saying drinking less is simple. There are constant opportunities to drink in many aspects of our lives.

Questions start to arise. What is considered lots of drinking? I thought 1-2 drinks a day could have medicinal value. What if I only drink on weekends? Are two drinks every night at 6 PM an acceptable reward, as I always feel fine the next day? If two drinks turn into 3 or 4, does that matter? This process is self-justification and convinces us that our current alcohol use is acceptable and fine. These questions and justifications of consumption really never end and will be customized to the individual. As with any drug, each person reacts differently to alcohol. What is considered a normal or small amount for one individual could be the hangover of the century for another. This reasoning is why I designed a 'one size fits all' approach to alcohol that can be used for any person who wants to have more control and accountability for their drinking and improve their relationship with alcohol. The strategies and guidelines are the same for everyone, whether they drink 1-2 glasses of wine every Friday night or have six or more beers each evening after work and unlimited amounts on the weekend. This program can be used for anyone in any environment at any point in time.

I created Free 40 to educate others to reduce their alcohol consumption by creating better daily habits and improving awareness and accountability for decision-making while increasing mental toughness. Improvement will come in the way of achieving daily, weekly, monthly, and lifetime goals related to alcohol and will spill over to other facets of your life. Awareness will be gained on the effect an individual's choices have on themselves and others. This improvement of physical and mental wellness and reducing consumption will lead to becoming a better, if not the best, version of one's self. Accountability will be present by making the individual consider all aspects of their life before deciding if alcohol fits the big picture of what they are trying to achieve in the short and long term. By the end of the book, I want every reader to be able to unlock a superpower we all have—**control of self**.

I am asking for a 365-day commitment to complete this program. I need the reader to want to reflect and change their relationship with alcohol while creating a new drinking pattern. Every year, you can decide if another lap around the sun is aligned with your goals. Whether you complete this program for one year or continually renew year after year, I am confident in saying your alcohol consumption will be reduced forever, and your life will be improved. Once you complete Free 40, the accomplishment can never be taken away from you and successfully completing a year of Free 40 is a great achievement that requires a high level of discipline and willpower. Remember, you have to want this. You have to want to accomplish this goal. You have to choose to execute daily. This goal is entirely on you to complete.

Free 40 is not a time-consuming, stretched-out read. I angled to try and get the book done in 40-80 pages with some worksheets to keep with the theme and importance of the number forty, which we will touch on later. I envision people re-reading a certain chapter or section of the book when presented with a potential drinking obstacle.

Everyone has super busy lives with many important tasks to complete, but this is one of the simplest yet challenging tasks one could accomplish, especially an individual who has been drinking weekly for years. Simplicity is the long-term goal, and once you begin living the Free 40 life, simplicity you shall achieve as your new relationship with alcohol has been established. You may even find controlling your alcohol use to be effortless.

Repetition and repetitive language, actions, and thoughts are very important in establishing personal growth and change. Going to the gym once won't grow the massive biceps you've been working on. You will find a very present layer of repetition as the book moves on. I want the readers to remind themselves of the core steps, motives, and actions needed to be successful with Free 40. The repetitive language in this book and in your personal day-to-day operations referring to alcohol consumption will help you drink less.

Another goal is that the reader will use this book as a reference guide, a playbook, or a tool as their journey for self-development continues and their relationship with alcohol and consumption changes for the better. There will be some data collection and mental training as we navigate through the book. I want alcohol use to be special again, as for many of us, drinking has become far too routine. My mission and main objectives are simple: Drink Less. Be Aware. Improve your Life.

Chapter 1:
Meet Aaron

My name is Aaron. I am a Canadian father of three who had drunk alcohol on a nearly weekly basis since Grade 10. I grew up in rural Southern Ontario and alcohol, like at many high schools, was a big part of my school's social culture. Around age 18, I began focusing on future goals, including attending college and university, and over the next five years, I had much success completing courses at these schools before graduating with a diploma and then a degree. Life was going well and my relationship with alcohol during these 5 years was controlled and possibly 'normal' by society's standards for young Canadian adult students. I worked five nights a week for the two years I was in college and only drank once or twice a week. While in university, this number went up to possibly an average of three times a week. I felt good during this time, exercised regularly, and passed all my classes with acceptable grades.

I began my professional career working with people who had mental illness and had acquired brain injuries.

After seven years, I transitioned into business and accepted an outside sales position working for an oil and fuel company. My curiosity and interest in people led to these opportunities being presented to me.

Over the next 14 years, I met my wife, evolved professionally, and had three sons. My oldest was born in January 2015, and then the twins arrived in May 2017. From a family perspective, I had accomplished so much, with more to come. I was, and remain, very excited about my sons' future and the active role I can play in it. However, there were issues that were beginning to become noticeable to me. Why was I not feeling more fulfilled by family life? The old clichés about boys being more work than girls and any failings as a parent myself seemed to be built-in cop-outs. Saying this is only temporary, it is normal to be tired and burned out after a long day of work and parenting, had become all too common. Was this really true? I felt like a near-completed puzzle that was missing some pieces. My awareness began to grow, and I knew improvements could be made.

Connecting with people has never been a problem for me as I have a vast social and professional network with hundreds of positive relationships with family, old and new friends, clients, co-workers, and members of my community. More questions started to emerge in my mind about my connectivity. Why am I not as enthusiastic or engaged when communicating with my network? I found myself being less in the moment with important people and my quality of conversation and focus was not there. Being a very enthusiastic, energetic person naturally, I was unsure if people noticed or if perhaps they chalked it up to me being tired from raising young boys and my busy lifestyle. Maybe hardly anyone noticed a difference because I was able to present myself well. Why did I keep accepting mediocrity? I knew I needed to be better, but why was I not getting anywhere?

Over the past five years, my weight was floating in the 250 to 260 lb. range, with a few peaks in the 270s and valleys in the 230s, which had me asking questions. What was I doing during these times of lower and higher weight that could have contributed to these numbers? The more I reflected, the more I realized alcohol was more and more of a culprit in my failings. By the end of 2019, I decided to start deliberate strategies to curtail my drinking.

In January 2020, I attempted a goal of not drinking for the entire month. I made it to 13 days and then had a beer. I had failed but flipped the script and said I would only drink on weekends for the remainder of the year, a tactic that had served me as a young adult. Why did I always find a path that still included drinking at a high frequency? While that goal went well, by the time Covid-19 arrived in March with schools shut down, things changed. Suddenly I was daddy day care, working from home, and consuming alcohol every night. We are talking as little as three but as many as ten drinks a night. This was the scary part. I was able to pull it off! Other than weight gain, the work was done, the kids were educated and cared for, and we made it through the summer. In reality, I was drowning in a lifestyle of consumption and denial. This was problematic drinking in full effect.

In Summer 2020, I decided to try another approach. I would give myself vouchers for the remainder of the year. I had ten vouchers a month, three had 1-3 drinks, three had 3-6 drinks, and four had 6+ drinks. Surely, this would work. Well, it did not, and I blew through those vouchers, and within three months, I was not tracking at all anymore. I drank every day in November and December 2020. I estimate in 2020, I drank up to 300 days. This was by far the most alcohol I had ever consumed in one year. A far cry from the 19-year-old version of myself who maybe drank 100 times a year, which is still very high. I think it should be noted and relatable that the 19-year-old version of anyone typically has less responsibilities than a 39-year-old version and physically should recover faster from alcohol. Father Time is undefeated, after all, so, in theory, one may think you would drink less as you age. That was not the case with me, as my alcohol consumption gradually went up and up. I exercised five days a week, took care of the kids, worked eight or more hours a day and got everything I needed done. Mind you, I was completely shot and lethargic by the end of the day. I had become a full-functioning, problematic drinker. This way of life was not sustainable. What was I going to do to change?

I began thinking about a streak I had attempted in 2003. My goal was to not drink for an entire month after a rough New Year's Eve. I made it 25 days, then after walking home from my friend's house, I stumbled by a birthday party of another friend, and I broke my streak. I then asked myself, when was the last time you went 30 days without alcohol? I could not remember and estimate, probably in Grade 9, in the fall of 1996. I recalled dozens of 1-2 weeks of breaks with no alcohol, but 30 days. That just did not happen. My relationship with alcohol was so strong that I could not recall a month's break since I was 14 years old.

I got down to work and said enough was enough. Covid-19 was another cop-out/built-in excuse for drinking and I did not want to have that crutch anymore. I got down to work and started some serious reflecting about why I drank. My relationship with alcohol had been inconsistent in the sense that some periods were very manageable and associated with fun and great memories, while others involved negative experiences or using alcohol to cope with a problem. The light bulb started flickering. Did I have most of my fun and memorable times with alcohol?

Two questions popped up. Did I know how to have fun the majority of the time without alcohol? Was alcohol actually making challenging times easier and more manageable or worse? I had been drinking so frequently for the past 25 years that I could not answer these questions in good faith. I needed to clear the slate and run a social experiment. The subject would be me, and I would monitor my alcohol use and my overall performance in my many daily roles, including husband, worker, father, and friend. I had been spinning my wheels for years, trying to plan on the fly and justify whatever decisions I had made. That was not going to happen anymore. I needed to figure out who I was without alcohol.

Chapter 2:
The Mission Begins

In January 2021, I was enjoying the Buffalo Bills playoff run. I am a Dallas Cowboys fan, but being 90 minutes from Buffalo has made them my default second-favorite team for years. I had enjoyed some beer and whisky during their first playoff game, which they won. I knew I wanted to start my journey soon, so I set the start date the day after the Bills playoff run ended. Their last game was on January 24. On January 25, I woke up hung over on a cold winter Monday morning and stepped on my scale. 275 lbs! This was the heaviest I had ever weighed, and I knew seeing this number was a blessing in disguise, as being 25 lbs. away from 300 lbs proved to be an excellent Day One starting point.

I had considered sobriety, but at that moment, I decided that option was not what was best for me. What I wanted was to significantly reduce the amount I drank when I drank, create scenarios that were acceptable for me to drink, and create a new standard for personal alcohol use. These factors would create a revamped and better relationship for myself with alcohol. I do believe that alcohol is not inherently evil and should not be stigmatized and labeled as bad. I wanted to create a new system where I could control extended periods of time without consumption, and when I chose to drink, certain measures or thresholds would be put in place.

As the days progressed, I began to notice almost instantaneous changes. My energy levels within three days were significantly better as my productivity went through the roof. I contributed more to my household duties and was able to have more, if not the same amount of work conversations, but there was a difference. I KNEW my customers and clients were getting a fully present, focused, and committed worker who was ready to serve them and not a tier-two mediocre nobody. I felt elevated.

I began tracking my calories and made a commitment to exercise seven days a week for a minimum of 30 minutes. Gyms were closed due to Covid-19 restrictions in Ontario, so I improvised by going for jogs and walks in my community, doing exercise videos on YouTube, skiing, and more. The sense of pride and accomplishment I experienced at the end of each day was hard to describe. I had not felt this way for this many consecutive days for as long as I could remember. I was stacking daily wins and becoming more mentally tough.

I had decided this initial hiatus would be 40 days. The days flew by, and I felt amazing. March 5th hit, and I was over 25 lbs lighter, mentally stronger, much happier, and so proud of this accomplishment I had not completed for 25 years. Free 40 had been working for me. A Transformation was underway. I committed on January 25, 2021, to live my life on more accountable and reflective terms to ensure I grow to my fullest potential and give not just myself but everyone I encounter for the rest of my life a better and evolving version of myself. The journey continues. Let me break down this system that has changed my life.

Chapter 3:
Why Quarantena (40 Days)

I began wondering how long my initial break from alcohol could be. A month seemed too standard, and 60 days was strongly considered. Then, I had a revelation as the universe showed me exactly how long my hiatus should be. I was researching the origins of the word quarantine and found this information.

"The word *quarantine* comes from ***Quarantena***, meaning **"forty days,"** used in the Venetian language in the 14th and 15th centuries. The word is designated in the period during which all ships were required to be isolated before passengers and crew could go ashore during the Black Death plague."

Wow. There it was. During a global pandemic, I was attempting to quarantine myself from alcohol. What a fantastic fit! This connection really excited me. I decided to name this program Free 40. I am a huge fan of double entendre and Free 40 is exactly that. My encouragement for alcohol consumption, should you choose to continue drinking after your initial 40-day break, is to only drink up to 40 times a year. Free 40 for consuming and NOT consuming alcohol.

I want the readers of this book to view these next 40 days as a transformation period. Whether the analogy is putting a fresh color of paint on an old house or moving to a new city with the ambition of a renewed start, Free 40 is a mindset of self-development, personal reflection, and improvement. You will transform into a vastly different person by the end of this initial cycle. I promise you after feeling the sense of euphoria and accomplishment the completion of the initial 40 days provides, you will never go back to a life of limitless, unaccountable alcohol use.

Chapter 4 (Ty): Free Forty

We all live busy lives and frankly, many people may not have the time to read and study this book multiple times. So, on one page, here is the entire phase 1 of Free 40 and a single line on phase 2.

Primary Goal

1. Do not drink alcohol for 40 consecutive days.

Optional Secondary Goals

2. Sleep a minimum of six hours a night.

3. Exercise 20 to 60 minutes a day, indoors or outdoors.

4. Cut out Late Night Snacking. Try not to eat anything after 8 PM.

5. Add anything else you feel could be of value, including reading, stretching, course work, time with family, or learning a new skill or hobby.

Phase 2

Drink alcohol up to 40 times the remainder of the year.

This is a most basic and quick write-up on 'Refrain Mode' and 'Indulge Mode'. Indulge Mode, the accountable consumption phase of Free 40, will be discussed later in the book.

I added the other optional non-alcohol-related steps to this program after noticing all these areas were neglected due to over drinking, and I had lost a degree of control over them. Eliminating and then changing your relationship with alcohol will be the catalyst that makes all the other personal goals more attainable and manageable. I am guessing that readers of this book could be complimented with various degrees of struggle related to sleep, eating, diet, exercise, and mood as a direct correlation to alcohol use. With Free 40, we give alcohol the most attention to changing without diminishing the importance of the other goals. I believe these secondary goals will just be the proverbial icing on the cake and much easier to manage once alcohol use is under control. You can feel confident and comfortable improving them as you move along. As mentioned, please customize and add as many secondary goals as you see fit.

My apologies for sounding like a broken record here, but I want all readers to take a deep look, study themselves, and reflect on how they use alcohol. I believe many people will see there are certain patterns associated with alcohol consumption and flipping the script on those patterns and changing your relationship with alcohol ultimately leads to your life changing or evolving for the better.

The steps listed seem very easy and in essence, they are. But we all know that actions speak much louder than words and decades-long habits, rituals, and ways of life take time, discipline, and dedication to break.

You can stop reading here; just do these steps and be successful, although I highly recommend reading the detailed breakdown of the who, what, where, when, why, and how of Free 40 to understand the system in greater detail.

Chapter 5:
The Captain of the Team: Alcohol

Alcohol loosens people's inhibitions and hinders productivity and willpower. Ever wonder why laying on the couch and eating bad foods all day is so conducive after a night of heavy drinking? This is an example of why, when unaccountable drinking is happening, alcohol becomes captain of the team. As team captain, he tells our sleep they don't need to put in as much time and can be minimized and unsettled. Alcohol then encourages our appetite to overeat, not feel full and crave salt, fatty, or sugary foods. What a leader! He's not done yet. Our captain then tells our mood to stop being so nice and rallies irritability, distraction, and depression to get their reps in at the gym while happiness, focus, and joy hit the showers. As for motivation and movement? Not today, pal. Our captain makes those wear ankle weights and if they are in the game, functioning will be much harder. Our captain is sneaky as initially, he is presented as a fun- loving, feel-good time, but we have learned better. One evening of over indulging leads to a day, maybe more, of recalibrating and getting alcohol off the field and back to the locker room.

Chapter 6:
The Compromise

"Absolutely! You are successful, popular and able to drink everyday. You deserve this drink, Cheers!"

Enters Mr. Red—a peer pressuring, freedom loving, supporter of enjoying casual beers anytime, anyplace and anywhere.

Mr. Blue is more science and accountability driven with alcohol. 100 years ago he would have been considered a dry and likely voted for prohibition.

Absolutely not! It's Thursday night. Alcohol hurts your body and mind. You should become sober or risk an earlier death.

Are these the only ways?

His friends and family drink every weekend. He has fun when drinking. Life is tough and alcohol helps him relax. Don't control his freedom.

20

21

The cartoon shown above is a humorous and relatable series of images illustrating how any individual could think about their drinking and the option of complete sobriety. On one shoulder, we see a cool, handsome, slick, assertive, and confident border lining on a cocky and arrogant man in red, encouraging our person to make no adjustments to their alcohol use. Everything is fine, you are doing well, have earned this status of enjoying alcohol, and indulge as much as you want with zero accountability. On the other shoulder, we have a man in blue, straight-faced, shaking their head, having reviewed your history, assessed your present, and looked into the crystal ball of the future to conclude you must stop drinking immediately and forever. Sobriety is the only way!

You are failing your family, not being the best worker, damaging your reputation in the community, getting gradually unhealthier, and creating a destiny of mediocrity, missed potential, and an early grave. A guarantee of mood issues connected to depression, anxiety, self-loathing, and self-doubt is absolute should you continue down this shameful path of alcohol abuse! The shame and judgment of the man in blue are unescapable.

The question is now asked: how do I act? Is alcohol this polarizing that I, as an individual, am either a slave of alcohol or pledge to sobriety for eternity? Is there no other way? Then a third person, A man in gold, presents himself in front of our conflicted person and points to Door Number Three, who was in the room all along but went unnoticed and said, "Let me show you another way." Mr. Blue and Mr. Red are shocked, their jaws dropping in contempt and disgust before seemingly fading from existence. Mr. Gold speaks up,

"Let's talk about another method and have you master skills you've possessed all along."

Free 40 is here for the other 90%.

Chapter 7:
Who and Hats

As individuals, we all wear many hats in a day. Awareness of how your hat changes from sunrise to sunset is very important to gain insight into all our different roles. Here's an example. Mike wakes up every morning at 6 AM and sets his family's clothes out before preparing breakfast. He has a conversation with his wife about an upcoming garden repair and is asked to get pricing from several businesses in the community for the job. After dropping his kids off at the bus stop and kissing his wife goodbye, he heads to his business, Free 40 Transportation, where he is part owner and lead manager.

Throughout the day, he has many discussions with co-workers about logistics and marketing strategies. Mike wants to be known as the transportation expert of his community and shares information on various social media platforms, including Facebook, Instagram, Twitter, and LinkedIn. He coordinates an order with his brake supplier before scheduling several hauls and deliveries. Mike leaves work and gets a 45-minute workout in at the gym. While on the treadmill, he speaks with Karen, who is concerned about the placement of new soccer fields in their town. They are too close to hydro towers, she claims. Mike hears her out in an empathetic fashion and suggests she write a letter to the mayor addressing her concerns.

Mike goes home and greets his family, helps make dinner with his wife before reviewing homework, and does some light play with the kids. Mike is part of his oldest son's baseball team, and they have an 8:30 PM practice. Mike and his wife Krista do a high five, and she nods when asked if she is able to put the younger two boys to bed. The practice goes well. Mike returns home and reads a quick book to his son before doing some final measurements of the garden renovation he is getting quotes on. His neighbor Doug is just bringing in his sprinkler. Mike says to Doug, "Your lawn is looking great." Doug nods with approval before going back inside as Mike starts to unwind and watches some TV before going to bed.

In this short scenario, you see a person who is wearing many hats in one day and constantly changing out of different roles with varying responsibilities. These include parent, spouse, business owner, worker, supplier, friend, coach, teammate, community member, neighbor, mentor, social media influencer, and entrepreneur. We are all constantly changing hats and need to build awareness of all the different hats we wear in a single day, as this alertness will help us be the best version of ourselves in each scenario. Whether you use alcohol or not, evaluating each hat and asking yourself, "How can I improve wearing this hat?" is bound to create improved success. Asking yourself how alcohol is affecting each of these hats may cause an eternal lightbulb to come on and ask, "How can I change this?" Let's review this scenario again with the possible presence of excessive alcohol use.

Mike has hit the snooze button of his alarm clock three times and is greeted by the sound of an overwhelmed wife and kids running around, hungry and needing some morning attention. Mike thinks to himself, did I have 5, 6, or 7 whiskies last night? Did I go to bed at Midnight or 1 AM? I can't quite remember. With alcohol on his breath and an extremely dry mouth, Mike makes his way downstairs and starts rushing to make breakfast. His wife is yelling at one of the kids for making a mess, and Mike stubs his toe, not paying attention to a stool that was left in the middle of the floor. "Have you thought about the garden repair, Mike?" his wife asks in a direct way, which requires an immediate response. "I keep forgetting. I promise I will do that today." "You have been saying that for a week." Mike is annoyed with that response and feels his wife should not be having a negative conversation with him this early in the morning. "Let's talk about this later." Krista reluctantly agrees as she shoves crackers in a bag and tells the boys to eat them in daddy's car. Mike then realized he had forgotten to fill his gas tank the previous evening! He wanted to do this the previous day but pushed it back due to being very tired after a long day of work and another poor night's sleep. You see, two nights ago, Mike had 3 or 4 drinks watching the hockey game and lost the ambition to fill his tank and worried that 3 or 4 drinks might put him in jeopardy of getting charged for a DUI. We will give Mike a style point for that insight!

Krista is fuming. "You are a mess today! Our day is completely thrown off." Mike pivots and suggests they switch cars. Krista agrees and he takes the kids to school, arriving with only two minutes to spare. "We made it!" Mike says proudly to himself. Even with a few late nights, I still have the magic touch and get the job done! Mike makes his way to work and is greeted by some inquiries from co-workers. Oh great, Chuck is complaining about that account again, Mike yells. "Chuck, Fox Inc is a terrible customer, who cares what they think, just tell them that we will get there when we get there." Chuck does not agree with this response but acknowledges and follows through. Mike attempts to sign on to his social media platform, but for some reason, the password is not working. "Damn it!" he yells, a co-worker who is on the phone with another customer; both hear the cursing.

Mike becomes irritable and says this project can wait. He then thinks to himself how his staff should be doing more, and they are to blame for the delay in their social media presence. Mike elects not to chat with his colleagues about marketing strategies and isolates himself in his office, where he sends emails and makes and returns phone calls. He pulls it off, places some orders and guts out the rest of the day. Four hours feel like 40. He sends one last email and notices a huge spelling error right after it was sent. "Oh well," he thinks before leaving the office very quickly with rapid goodbyes.

Mike is way too tired for a workout. *I went twice last week,* he thought, *tomorrow will do. I'll give my body a day to rest.* Good planning, Mike thinks. Mike goes home, greets his family, and suggests they just microwave some leftovers and eat Kraft dinner. He does not feel like making a 'big dinner' and does not want the leftovers to go to waste. Krista starts talking to him about her day, but he really isn't present in the moment. He hears her words, but they don't mean anything to him. This moment reminds him of his conversations with customers earlier today. He is floating through another conversation on autopilot. I am good at giving people my attention, Mike thinks. Krista agrees to put the kids to bed and reminds Mike of the baseball practice. Mike gets his son ready and drives to the field in his gassed-up vehicle, which his wife filled for him.

Mike has a craving for fast food, likely due to not eating a very filling dinner and whips into Mcdonald's. The server seems new and there is a delay in getting Mike his burger. He becomes angry and scolds the teenager for a bad job and says it's his fault they are late for baseball practice. Mike and his son arrive four minutes late and start going through the motions. The coaching staff asks Mike how he is doing, and he falls back into the coast mode, saying traditional expressions like "steady as she goes," "live to fight another day," etc. The other coaches seem to be taking the lead and Mike has to leave practice once midway through to use the bathroom. Seems that McDonald's did not agree with him, and he should have known whenever he eats fast food after drinking whisky, his stomach issues are all but guaranteed. The practice ends and Mike and his son hear one of the other players say, "go to sleep, Mr. Mac, you're shot!"

Mike returns home, sends his son to bed, and decides to put off doing his first measurement of the garden renovation he is getting quotes on. "That can wait till tomorrow, I am going to bed soon," Mike tells himself confidently. Mike starts to unwind, watches some TV and notices that an old movie is on he really enjoys. I will stay up for the last 45 minutes. Mike looks around his house, which seems extra messy and thinks his family needs to pitch in more; he's doing everything. He notices on his counter sits the bottle of whisky he forgot to put away, with about 2-3 ounces left in it. "Might as well finish it off," he thinks as he pours himself what is one very stiff drink! The bottle is now empty, and Mike throws it in the garbage can, too tired and lazy to put it in the recycling bin in the garage. Mike sits down and continues watching his movie as he has his first sip and voices a "yum" as he enjoys the complex flavor of this rare bourbon. I will just have one and then head to bed. Funny, Mike said that to himself the past two nights.

As you can see, this same individual had two very different outcomes. My position is the presence and use of too much alcohol was the primary reason his second day was so challenging. Some key problems I noticed with Mike in scenario two while using alcohol poorly included the following: A severe lack of motivation and sleep problems, not staying in the moment and giving people and situations his full attention, memory challenges, constant and habitual excuse-making, justification and blaming, physical problems, relationship struggles, reputation issues, mediocre work abilities, clumsiness, weak communication, poor reactionary skills and the addictive nature of alcohol.

I encourage everyone to spend some time and reflect on how many hats they are wearing in a day, week, or month. These will be different and customized to each individual. Review your daily hats and ask, "How can reducing alcohol use make wearing these hats easier and make me a better individual?"

Chapter 8: Where

ANYWHERE you are present. Be mindful of certain 'where's' that may have an association with alcohol, and cautiously but optimistically evaluate why this location is correlated with drinking. Mentally review how many 'where's' you have given yourself permission to drink alcohol in. Is it too many? Are they similar? What are the consistencies of where I drink? By organizing your thoughts and determining the where of alcohol use, you will be able to better evaluate if these locations meet your evolving threshold for consuming alcohol and if some need to be eliminated.

During this, you may discover there are some evident consistencies where you use alcohol. These could include consuming at a similar location, at specific times, and with specific people. Ask yourself, are these locations triggers for alcohol use, and if so, why? **Does having alcohol in these locations add value to my experience?** Do I typically always have three glasses of wine on Tuesday evenings while marking papers in my office? Is the environment I am in a net positive or negative location for drinking?

Chapter 9: When

Free 40 can start at any point for any individual. The first stage of the system involves abstaining from alcohol for 40 consecutive days. There is NO flexibility in this phase. This can be challenging, and it took me 25 years to go over a month without alcohol. You may want to consider gradually building up your confidence and reducing your alcohol intake before jumping in headfirst. Each of us will have a different 'when.' The choice of when you start is yours.

During this initial phase, I encourage you to document and reflect on how the days have been. You can keep notes on your phone a journal, or fill in a calendar, whichever method works best for you. I wrote down 1 to 40 on my calendar, and as each day passed, I crossed off a number. Keep a mental inventory of what feels differently and how these 40 days are distinct from others. I will include an option example of a tracking worksheet you could use during this phase at the end of the book.

There is no flexibility in this initial phase of Free 40. To be successful, you must not have alcohol for 40 consecutive days. I know you can do this. I will be waiting for you at the end of the line. On Day 41, think of me as being your biggest supporter, throwing high fives and praise your way. The process can and WILL be very challenging for most people who drink at a minimum, even occasionally. Forty days is a long time. Hold the course. Once this 40-day hiatus is completed, it is an accomplishment that can never be taken away from you. Like getting your name carved on the Stanley Cup or attending The Masters Final Round in Augusta, the lifestyle change will be with you forever, whether acknowledged on a conscious or subconscious level. Your mind and soul will know you can control any personal goal that you have strived for. You can do this!

Chapter 10:
What and the ABCs of Free 40

Circling back to an early section of the book, here are the main primary goals of the book and some optional secondary goals.

Primary Goal

Do not drink alcohol for 40 consecutive days.

Optional Secondary Goals

Sleep a minimum of 6 hours a night: Our bodies need time to heal and recharge. Alcohol seriously affects sleep quality, and an awareness about achieving better sleep is needed. Once gained, it could catapult you to recognize that alcohol will almost certainly negatively affect this aspect of your life if overused.

Exercise 20 to 60 minutes a day indoors or outdoors. Movement and exercise offer many health benefits. Be aware of how much more manageable your productivity is during these workouts in the absence of alcohol.

End late-night snacking. Once you have your last bite of the day, do not eat anything until the next morning. This system helps give your digestive tract a break and works to eliminate late-night snacking. Be aware that drinking alcohol in the evening could lead to late-night eating. This method, I believe, has been a big factor in my ongoing weight loss and current state of health and wellness. I have ulcerative colitis and my doctor has supported and encouraged me to give my digestion track this daily break. Don't expect perfection and if you are hungry, please, by all means, eat!

I wanted to briefly expand on some of the benefits of these points and want my readers to understand and reinforce that not drinking for 40 consecutive days is the only mandatory goal of these steps. I added these other goals as you will find they all become much easier to attain when alcohol is reduced from your life. I truly do not want any readers or active members of Free 40 to feel any negative emotions, have poor sleep, or miss a workout. You still are being successful if these steps are not completed. Not drinking for 40 consecutive days is the ONLY set-in-stone goal that has to be completed to pass this first phase of the program. The other steps are optional.

The ABCs of Free 40

I love acronyms. They help me remember many different thoughts and ideas. The ABCs have to be one of our personal foundational memory acronyms. We've used it since we were children. In the Free 40 context, ABC stands for the following: Awareness, Balance, and Control.

Awareness: To be aware that one wants to improve their relationship with alcohol and acknowledge alcohol can have harmful effects.

Balance: To practice a life that includes a balanced approach to alcohol consumption and day-to-day responsibilities.

Control: To control one's decision-making with alcohol use and be accountable for what one drinks. Drink with a plan and be in control.

Chapter 11:
Why-The Most Important Feature

This is the most individualized component of Free 40, as everyone's reasoning for why they want to change their relationship with alcohol will be different. I would like to share some of my 'Why' reasons for sticking with Free 40. You are more than welcome to customize your 'why' as you go through the program.

Life Expectancy:

I have a personal goal of living an active life and becoming a supercentenarian, which means an individual living to the age of 110. My goal number is 117, as I want to see the turn of the next century on January 1, 2100. With growing life expectancy and ever-changing and evolving breakthroughs with AI preventive medicine, genetics and aging, and curing diseases like cancer, medical science is going to be on our side. What can we do to complement these benefits? Work on being a better version of yourself and keep a positive mental state with healthier body composition. As a former 275-pound male, I did not notice any people closing in on 100 who were remotely close to this weight. The odds of reaching this high number will be improved with healthier lifestyle habits, including limiting alcohol. I read an article stating that in 2100, there will be at least one person born in 1970 who's still alive at age 129, turning 130. I was born in 1982. Why not me?

Role Modeling/Improving Community:

By making this lifestyle change, you will become a pillar of hope for anyone else who is having struggles and wants to experience self-improvement and control of self. This is not limited to someone just wanting to evaluate and change their relationship with alcohol. They may want to change their diet, become more physically active or happier, or be more positive in life. The sky truly is the limit on how your actions will positively impact everyone you touch. Making a positive impact in someone's life is one of the greatest gifts we can give another individual. Serving others is the greatest key to happiness.

Increased Daily Motivation and Productivity:

Alcohol serves as an anchor to many people's ability to get motivated and work towards their daily, weekly, and long-term goals. I often justified my current position and decisions to drink due to perceived and inflated positives about my life. My ego needed to be checked, and my awareness, including exaggerating my success in most situations, was becoming clear. Drinking too frequently promotes 'Increased Daily Mediocrity.' Less productive work takes place, and this is a net negative. Sure, you can probably pull these days off and get by with a 5/10 productivity level, but deep down in your heart of hearts, you know you could have done so much better. Consistent alcohol use prevents us from being our most motivated and positive selves.

Elevated Mood:

Elevated moods are another point that often gets scapegoated to other facets of life, including stress, poor sleep, and interpersonal conflict. These areas can drastically affect our mood. Alcohol simply does not make these life challenges any easier and undoubtedly worsens each situation. Making a focus on an elevated mood, being a primary 'why' of Free 40, is highly recommended for any participant of the program. Watch how more manageable mood-affecting actions and scenarios play out once alcohol consumption is reduced. I guarantee this, above all else, will be the biggest lock for personal growth once the relationship with alcohol is lessened. You will be a happier person!

Better and More Precise Communication:

Words and language matter and will so more than ever as we move forward in a time where people have never had the ability or opportunity to be so connected to one another. Connectivity will continue to grow, and it is in our best interests to have high-level communication skills. Alcohol is a neurotoxin and scientifically is shown to have adverse effects on your brain, which in turn affects language and communication. The brain's chemistry changes. I have recently heard of the term brain atrophy to describe the state of your brain when too much drinking has happened (How scary is that concept!) Conversation and language can be very precise and exciting. Evaluating the whole body of work after drinking tells a different story. Many people's ability to communicate lessens the more they drink as this initial euphoric stage of alcohol wears off. The following day can be excruciatingly difficult to have high-quality conversations and messaging. I am sure many of you are quite good at pulling off lots of high-quality dialogue the day after drinking, but I suspect this process could have been much easier if less drinking and better sleep had occurred. Comparing how you communicate and the language used after days of alcohol consumed to days when there has been no alcohol will show a noticeable difference.

Accountability:

One personal goal I have kept myself extremely accountable for is evaluating all the factors in place before I decide to have a drink. Am I in a safe environment? Do I have a plan to get home? What is my personal responsibility level in the now and the future? These questions and decisions made after evaluation will help create personal accountability. Alcohol has consequences. Ask someone how many days they drank last month, and I doubt many can give a firm and accurate answer. I can now. Drinking has become second nature in Western culture. This personal relationship many have with alcohol deserves a strong evaluation.

Once an emphasis on accountable drinking and personal responsibility has been established, less alcohol consumption in more appropriate scenarios will occur.

This will be a natural progression of you keeping yourself accountable for what you drink. Not only will this element be added to alcohol, but you may notice other areas of your life involved with work, family, social, and your community will improve or become better as your awareness and commitment to personal accountability grows. After being aware of how your accountability has impacted those around you, a progressive desire to maintain these levels for others and positive expectations of yourself will add another important level of accountability.

Environmental Awareness/Heightened Senses:

Reducing drinking will allow an individual to be more aware of their environment while fine-tuning and advancing their senses, including smell, touch, sight, taste and sound. As the program evolves, make a conscious effort to document or discuss how this occurs. Some examples could include smells being more enticing to stimulate appetite as opposed to making you nauseous, music or the sound of people becoming calming instead of causing a headache or irritation, food tasting much better without risk of stomach discomfort after consumption, and sights and images created leaving you feeling more fulfilled or curious, instead of bland neutrality and boredom. The neurotoxin dulls senses and after regulating your alcohol consumption, these areas of everyday life become much more noticeable and enjoyable to experience.

Being Present:

Our attention is needed almost continuously throughout the day in a variety of capacities. How often have you been half-checked out when having a conversation with a loved one or co-worker? Are you doing your best to avoid human contact and conversation when grocery shopping because of a hangover, or is alcohol contributing to you not having a shower or wearing clean clothes? Do you avoid social events and community gatherings because of a general feeling of discomfort? This could all be a result of too much or unregulated alcohol consumption, which hinders one's ability to stay present in the moment.

I want to beat the drum as loudly as I can to encourage all readers of this book to monitor how deep and meaningful their conversations and moments are with others when alcohol has been eliminated. We appreciate others more when a hangover is not present. Some studies have shown alcohol can stay in one's system in some capacity for as long as 80 hours. I will take high-quality conversations and memorable moments over liquor-fueled avoidance and annoyance any day!

Daily Pride and Sense of Achievement and Winning:

People do not give themselves enough credit for their daily accomplishments. Life with alcohol can become so routine and mundane that a sense of pride is not felt after a day's work if booze is part of the equation. There is this weird twist in logic where some people may feel that drinking at the end of their day is their sense of 'achievement.' I know this habit or ritual is unhealthy. By putting pen to paper or being mentally aware, whatever method works for you, each day making a commitment to not drinking and completing the other aspects of Free 40, you are assured to feel a sense of personal satisfaction and accomplishment. I am continually asking myself, "What in the next 24 hours can I complete to make these long-term goals a reality?" Not drinking and being productive is almost always part of the answer. You can do this too!

One of the biggest tactics to having dry days during Free 40 is making a daily commitment in the morning that you will not drink this day. This day-to-day approach works and is an important piece for people who practice and live sobriety. Every day you complete this affirmation is a huge win.

Every day you go without drinking is a huge moral and physical victory. Give yourself permission to win and achieve this goal daily. Completing not only the alcohol reduction component of Free 40 but also the other parts will give you a daily dose of gratification and accomplishment. You will win daily, and these victories will elevate and improve your life. And when the time is right to cash in some of your 40 vouchers for alcohol use, the drinks will feel more earned and justified. Just keep it under control.

Preparation and Performance:

Preparation is needed for activating our superpower of 'Control of Self.' Always ask yourself. What is the best method to achieve the most desired outcome. A pro athlete would complete customized exercise and training programs while studying film to give them the best opportunity for success and optimal performance. A fisherman would review what areas of the water he had the most success in, what equipment worked best for catching, and the best time of year to fish. Each profession and task in life has a degree of preparation. Some are so mundane as selecting what type of socks to put on to protect your feet for the day. We could drown in micromanaging every bit of preparation an individual will use in a day, so we won't go there. Focus your preparation on how to drink less.

This could include some of the following:

- Making a daily affirmation not to drink.
- Fill time that historically has been used for drinking with other tasks.
- Embrace a community of people to share your goals with that will create accountability. You will not want to fail these people by deviating from your goals. This could include a small group of friends, family members, or less personal communities such as AA or Recovery Elevator on Facebook/Websites.
- Limit the amount of alcohol kept in your house and keep beer at room temperature until drinking.
- Find substitutes like non-alcoholic beer or other beverages. I like Partake beer and find it has a placebo social effect in party/social situations. Sparkling Water and Shirley Temples have been excellent substitutes. A swish or gargle of liquor before spitting it out has helped address and reduce cravings.
- Create mini goals for each week or month regarding the amount of alcohol you want to consume. Circling back to a comment made a few points ago, the daily dose of

gratification and accomplishment as a result of following through with your prepared plan is an incredible feeling. Please reward yourself and acknowledge and embrace your daily successes as they occur. Don't be afraid to plan and execute three days of drinking on your holiday in Nashville or an all-inclusive resort in the Caribbean. Embrace the rewards of your hard work.

Your organization and preparation skills will ripple to other aspects of your life as the lack of regulated alcohol control and consumption was likely impeding your ability to prepare and perform in other aspects of life. Winners prepare... You're a winner!

Authenticity and Commitment:

Authenticity and commitment go hand in hand with your 'why.' By committing to this goal of controlled alcohol consumption, you are changing what your authentic self is. You are someone who drinks with accountability and is committed to maintaining this process and lifestyle habit. I feel if I am not following through on my yearly alcohol goal, my authenticity becomes counterfeit, and I lose out on checking the box on commitment. This is a point I do not want to underestimate, as failing here compromises the person I am striving to become.

Sleep:

Alcohol inhibits the body and mind from reaching optimal sleep and can disrupt sleep patterns. By limiting your alcohol consumption, you could improve not just the amount but the quality of your sleep. I personally feel getting under four hours of sleep can be worse than a hangover. I have dealt with poor sleeping patterns, irrespective of alcohol, for the majority of my adult life, and I have consulted a doctor in the past to receive medication, support, and strategies to improve my sleep. I would recommend that anyone else who is using alcohol to help improve sleep or has struggled with similar problems make an appointment with their family doctor to discuss different remedies.

Improve Immunity:

Post Covid-19 is likely the dawn of a new era of improving personal immunity to protect one's self from this disease or others like it.

Here is a list of suggestions on how one can improve immunity:

- Don't smoke.
- Eat a diet high in fruits and vegetables.
- Exercise regularly.
- Maintain a healthy weight.
- If you drink alcohol, drink only in moderation.

- Get adequate sleep.
- Take steps to avoid infection, such as washing your hands frequently and cooking meats thoroughly.

Free 40's plan touches most of these, so by the nature of completing and committing to the program, you will be increasing the likelihood of a stronger and improved immunity. I would encourage my readers to start visualizing improving immunity as another specific goal of the program. When you aren't sick, you are more productive, happy, and healthy, and the risk of infecting someone else goes down as well.

Chapter 12:
How

For this important section, let's first focus on how neuroplasticity works. Neuroplasticity is one of the crown jewels of Free 40, and it is changing behavior forever. Neuroplasticity is the brain's ability to reorganize itself by forming new neural connections in your brain, and with these new connections come different actions and behaviors.

As the legendary Dr. Jason Selk, author of *Relentless Solution Focus*, states, "Neurons that fire together wire together." As you navigate towards a life with less alcohol, healthier decisions, and more daily goals being achieved, your brain is adjusting and creating these new pathways, thus making this behavior a new habit and scientifically changing how you are wired." How cool is that? Free 40 is naturally helping these new pathways create themselves. I like to think of my brain as a computer that is being reprogrammed to be more efficient, effective, and better than before. A software update! Acknowledging how your mind is evolving can be rewarding in itself. Being aware of how this process is happening and recognizing the process while you undertake your personal transformation and growth is very satisfying.

Similar to the Why section, I will break down very specific ways and strategies on how to successfully complete Free 40. Executing these points daily will lead to triumph, and you will not fail if you follow these steps.

A Commitment to Execution:

Start with a commitment to go 40 days without alcohol and build from there. Commit every day for the first 40 days that you will not consume any alcohol. This is a regimented daily assignment and will create a scenario where you are executing a planned task every day. At the end of the day, enjoy your win and accomplishment.

Daily Affirmations:

Have a daily affirmation or pledge to your goal. Verbalize this goal. Write it down on a piece of paper. Jot it down in the notes of your phone. Tell a friend or family member. Be sure to say words along the lines of, "I am not drinking today." Self-talk works and saying what you plan on doing makes the goal more likely to happen. This is a manifestation of words to action. One of my favorite affirmations is The Serenity Prayer by American Theologist Reinhold Niebuhr, who said, "Give me the serenity to accept the things I cannot change, courage to change the things I can, and wisdom to know the difference."

Community of Like-Minded People:

Having a network of like-minded people to share your progress and success is very important. This could include online communities like Recovery Elevator, a platform where people from all over the world share their journeys of sobriety and life-changing habits with others. Other support groups could be formed. There are lots of them out there. Possibly consider starting your own if you have a network or group of people all trying to cut back on their drinking.

Reduce People Pleasing, Learn to Say "No":

Have acknowledgement of how 'people pleasing' and living a life with a lack of personal boundaries can lead to excessive drinking. For many of us, alcohol use has become synonymous with socializing. There are many questions or blowbacks about your decision not to drink as others could look at themselves and be uncomfortable that your decision to abstain is a passive-aggressive judgment of them. This is simply not correct and true friends should understand you are creating a healthier lifestyle to improve your world. I personally will use the lines, "I am dry today" or "I will take a rain cheque," when asked to have a drink, which is essentially true.

Boundary Setting:

Piggybacking from the last point, boundary settings are extremely important in all facets of life, not just with alcohol. By having a 40-day hiatus from alcohol and then committing to only drinking 40 times a year, you have chosen an extremely lengthy and rewarding personal boundary. Use an analogy of a telescope looking at a star, and you being the telescope and the star being your 365/40/40 day commitment. You want to get to this star in one year, which is a very broad and specific goal. Black and White. However, reaching this star will involve incremental daily, weekly, and monthly improvements around the times you will drink alcohol and, more so, times and opportunities that you will not. This flips the analogy of a telescope to a microscope, where, on a much more frequent basis, you are evaluating the scenarios you will drink alcohol in and asking yourself, "Will this decision prevent me from reaching my daily and yearly goal, and does having alcohol in this moment add value to my experience?" This process becomes second nature in time, and you will see that your standards or boundaries for having alcohol will become much higher than before. Before you know it, you have set foot on that star that initially seemed so far away. Your brain will be reprogrammed.

You could write down a daily checklist with your five goals of Free 40. Put a mark next to them when completed. Make sure the alcohol goal is checked EVERY DAY.

Prepare for a Variety of Reactions and Feedback:

This journey you are on will not gain full support or understanding from everyone in your social circle. At least not right away, and it could possibly never happen. Many individuals will not have or recognize this new boundary you have created with alcohol, and the idea of this concept could scare and upset them. People may refer to your decision as a cleanse or diet, a phase, or other words, to minimize what exactly you are trying to accomplish. Naturally, being a spectator to your transformation could make an individual self-reflect and this is not always enjoyable. Be aware you cannot control how someone else feels and acts. "Control the controllable" is a quote I like and the only things we can control are what we say, how we act and react, and how we feel.

Try not to be offended if people belittle or don't take your goal seriously, as you are doing this for yourself and to improve YOUR life. I would suggest if you sense certain people are not comfortable or supportive of your new lifestyle, do not spend much time telling them what you have accomplished so far. There are more appropriate people to celebrate with. Keep in mind that, more often than not, your behavior and decision-making hold a better chance of inspiring and motivating someone else to change their health and relationship with alcohol as opposed to just talking about the process. I had three friends go dry for 40 days within one month of my goal, and now they are committed to maintaining a more aware and accountable relationship with alcohol.

So, here is the slippery slope of this point. Be aware of whom to discuss your actions with, and do not preach or show your pride with someone who could be uncomfortable or uneasy with your goals. This is a very challenging balance to maintain, but it is possible!

Label Alcohol, Alcohol:

For all the creative, interesting, and distinctive ways alcohol is presented, at the end of the day, alcohol is still alcohol. My favorite bourbon, Weller 107, is alcohol. Beer is alcohol. Wine is alcohol. A tasty Pina Colada with a pineapple slice and a little umbrella on the beach in Cancun is alcohol! Start speaking in a manner where you talk along the lines of, "At Joe's poker game next Saturday, I am going to drink alcohol." Terms like having 'a few pops,' 'some casuals,' 'happy hour drinks,' etc., are, in my mind, a disservice to reaching your goal. Dissociating the concept of happy hour and casual pops from alcohol will make your goal easier to achieve, and your relationship with these drinks will become more controlled and manageable. Language and words matter.

Celebrate Mini and Major Milestones:

Whether it be a single day, 40 consecutive days, or a mini goal of going two weeks dry, be sure to celebrate this achievement. Making this fundamental life change with your relationship with alcohol is not easy and will be a daily and yearly goal to maintain. Adding celebration into your routine for when these goals are accomplished will bring out a heightened level of happiness within you that will be felt by others. High fives for everyone! Think of your excitement and joy as a light that brightens up every room it enters. And flipping the script, be sure to celebrate the days of the year you prepared and chose to drink alcohol. These days are part of your plan. Enjoy them. Cherish them. Personally, I have felt more rewarded for drinking on these days than ever before. I now finally feel I have earned the right to drink on a day, time, place, and with people I feel comfortable. I have full control over alcohol, and this is definitely worth celebrating! Alcohol consumption has become special for me again.

Become Obsessed:

Synonyms for obsession include passion and fixation. Obsession, if used correctly, can be a very powerful tool for achieving your alcohol goals. Perhaps you have never been extremely obsessed before. I believe there are degrees (mild-moderate-extreme) to this feeling, and extreme obsession in some areas becomes negative. We are using obsession as a tool to fully control and limit alcohol use, so in this goal, the feeling is positive. To become obsessed, spend time visualizing how you are going to complete your 365-day goal of 40 days dry and 40 days of consuming. Keep a mental note or, preferably, jot down in your phone or calendar target dates for streaks of not drinking. Be sure to remind yourself of these daily and affirm to yourself these are non-negotiable.

You could find a spot in your house or community that makes you feel laser-focused and go there as needed to reflect on how well your work and effort have been going. Spend time forecasting how much better your physical health, mental well-being, and overall life will be if you continue to hold this course and conquer your alcohol goals. What you are doing with this obsession is turning the process into a daily and long-term winning proposition. This obsession ends up not just being about reducing alcohol but winning in your day-to-day life all the time. Chasing wins ripples off into countless other aspects of your life and all of a sudden, before you know it, a higher level of achievement and standard is present everywhere you are. Obsession has been your best ally, and by using it to help change your alcohol use, this domino effect has occurred, which is now changing many aspects of your life in a positive direction forever. Obsession can equal winning.

Visualizing Personal Transformation:

Dopamine is the pleasure molecule in the brain that is activated when we dream, visualize, and begin to execute our goals. Visualizing daily what your life will look like when alcohol has been reduced will make that goal become more of a reality and help fire up the dopamine in your mind. The thought of having more energy due to better sleep after not drinking is not far from being a reality. Embrace how losing weight and being prouder of your body and physical health can be a reality if you visualize the steps it takes to get there. Do you feel mediocre?

Start visualizing how changing your relationship with alcohol will transform your body, mind, and soul to levels you never knew possible. Once you visualize these goals, decision-making will reflect these thoughts and actions and executions to achieve your visions start becoming second nature. Think positive thoughts and bring them to reality. You become your thoughts; your thoughts become you.

Visualize how your future self is selling your current self on an image of how your future can include so many new and rewarding opportunities. Get excited about what you are going to do with all the extra money you are saving from not drinking so much or what tasks you will complete with the extra energy you have from not being hungover. Get ready for the compliments from people who have not seen you for a while as they rave about how much weight you have lost or how you have changed, and they can't quite put their finger on why. This personal transformation, which is chock-full of consistent successes, becomes intoxicating. Imagine that being intoxicated on personal growth and success. How sweet is that?

Understand Your Wins and Keep Winning:

To achieve Free 40, you will string together countless wins. Winning will become part of your life and behavior. Your work life becomes more enjoyable and profitable. Your quality of friendship and personal relationships improve. You feel like a better member of your community. All these accomplishments and winning are much more enjoyable than frequent alcohol use. And here's the kicker: you can still win when you do drink! By drinking in such a limited and special occasion manner, these drinks become much more enjoyable, and you will feel the accomplishment and pride of winning when you do choose to drink. Winning and understanding how Free 40 is all about winning is crucial for optimal success in the program. Embrace your daily victories and be proud of your actions.

Create Friction with Alcohol:

Don't go pick a fight with an alcohol bottle, you might cut your hand. What I mean is make friction for when you do choose to drink. A non-drinking example could be going to bed in your workout clothes to promote a gym workout the following day. There is friction, you are taking off the clothes before your workout is complete. In the case of alcohol, try keeping beers at room temperature, wine and spirits in the garage and not easily accessible, or keep no alcohol in your house and go to a store to purchase booze when the moment arrives. Be focused on creating friction and watch your cravings diminish.

Ask Yourself-Why Not Me?

Why not you? Are you 21, 35, 42 or 63? Do you feel this shift in lifestyle is great, but you just aren't worthy of becoming a better you? Does being 'partially sober' or 'alcohol-free 90% of the time' make you feel unworthy, like an imposter? Why can't you change your current alcohol habits and start a chain reaction that improves your entire life? Why can't you be the first one in your family or circle of friends who acknowledge they are not the best they can be due to excess alcohol use and lead the way for others? Is there doubt about you being able to accomplish these goals? Of course, there is. All people have self-doubt about everything, but remember, you can do this! Any one of us can do this. Anyone can unlock their superpower of Control of Self.

The core of this book is in the who, what, where, when, why, and how of Free 40. These pages are your guidelines for daily reminders of the importance of the process and answers to almost anything you may have as the transformation continues. These chapters are motivation and fuel for your journey. This next section of the book offers different insights into the concept of committing to the Free 40 lifestyle.

Chapter 13:
Are You Wet or Dry?

Pre-Prohibition, the Western world was very divided on alcohol use and its role in society. The majority of people fell into two categories: Wets and Dries! Wets were individuals who believed alcohol should be consumed by any adult over the legal drinking age without consequence. This thinking aligns with our friend Mr. Red from the cartoon strip earlier in the book. Dries believed alcohol was inherently evil, morally wrong, damaged the social and moral fabric of society, and should be outlawed and banished forever. This mindset is in line with our pal from earlier in the book, Mr. Blue.

I feel confident saying both of these groups of people were way off on what was best for their communities. People deserve an opportunity to decide for themselves if they want to consume alcohol, and having the state completely outlaw alcohol was an approach that was destined to fail. I understand the intent of both groups as I believe they were coming from good intentions of doing what was best for their country and personal freedoms as individuals.

One hundred plus years of this binary quandary of 'to drink or not to drink,' 'to be dry or wet' continues. Free 40 offers a different approach. Anyone who commits to this system is neither wet nor dry, but up to 40 days a year is damp! Damp on their own terms, in full control, and without judgment. Wet and Dry is not how Free 40 works. Black and White thinking is out; let's maneuver in the grey.

Chapter 14: Support and Supportive Thinking

Not everyone may have a support network of like-minded individuals, close friends, or family members, or enough people to help encourage them. This is not an easy task; it is very hard but will get easier in time. For anyone who is anxious about not having enough support, I will be your support person. I will encourage you. I will be your springboard for bouncing off positive and negative experiences. I can be your champion and help guide you until the process and your transformation is completed and you become the best version of yourself! I fully believe every single person on the planet can complete this program and improve their lives for the better.

Be sure not to let past outcomes, including failures and mistakes, dictate your future. If anything, look at these mishaps as learning moments that have brought you to this very moment as you strive for a better you and greatness. Your personal evolution and transformation will never end.

Do not stay lost in the past. Tap into nostalgia temporarily, but only briefly while continually moving forward. I want your mindset to be 99% in the present and future.

One of my biggest takeaways and acknowledgments since this journey began is how I am evaluating and enjoying celebrations. Moments that may have been lessened by alcohol, like being hungover at my child's sporting event, have been elevated by booze having zero role in the experience. My presence and attention in these moments are higher, and the celebration for myself and those around me is greater. As for when I have had alcohol, those moments have been better than ever before. I feel a huge sense of accomplishment. The people I choose to be with and the moments we are celebrating feel better than ever. I believe this is due to the rewarding feeling of planning the outcomes and executing the plan to drink in a controlled manner while making the scenarios where I use alcohol more special. Dopamine is again at work doing its magic! There is no more Wednesday night six-pack during a hockey game, which most certainly leads to a midnight snack! Those events have gone completely extinct and will not return.

Chapter 15:
Let's Chat Indulge Mode

Here, we break down what situations, scenarios, environments, and circumstances will get your seal of approval to drink alcohol. These markers will be different for everyone. I believe there will be consistency throughout these days.

A Curve Ball, Want to be Sober Instead?

You have completed the initial 40 days of Free 40, and being alcohol-free has made you feel better than you have in years. You don't have to drink 40 days a year now to still complete this program. You may choose sobriety as your life path moving forward, and I could not be happier for you. I love and embrace the commitment to sobriety and look at anyone who has become sober as a hero. This is a very personal decision, and I would be remiss in a book about changing one's relationship with alcohol and living a life committed to planned and accountable drinking that sobriety was not suggested. I feel this path is best for some, and if this decision resonates with you, please follow your dreams and do what is best for yourself.

The Voucher System

I think of these indulging days as unusual and not standard for my day-to-day life. The re-creation of your relationship with alcohol will make drinking far less common and rare. As I navigated through the first year of Free 40, my friends would ask me if I was using a voucher on a given day at a certain event. I think labeling a day you drink as using a voucher is catchy, and frankly, I like saying, "It's a voucher day!" So, the vouchers have been synonymous with the indulgence portion of Free 40. You have 40 vouchers at your disposal for the rest of your journey. Choose and use them wisely and remember you have earned these.

You Don't Have to Drink 40 Days!

UP TO 40 days is the goal and maximum threshold for successfully completing this program. Remember, to successfully complete this program, an individual has to do two things. #1. Do not drink for 40 consecutive days. #2. Drink up to 40 days a year. Up to is the operative phrase here. I chuckle, thinking about someone who has been drinking 33 days by Christmas, looks at the year in review, and says, "Holy Moly, I have seven days of alcohol drinking left, time for a bender!" Please remind yourself that 33 days would be perfectly fine to complete the program still admirably. I love the idea of maxing out in life, but you don't need to use each of these 40 vouchers to be successful.

Chapter 16:
A New Way of Drinking: Indulge Mode

The fundamentals of indulge mode involve developing preparation, targets, markers, and thresholds that should be hit or met before you decide to drink. You are deliberately shifting your drinking habits and how you think about alcohol. Before, you may have just reached the fridge for a beer; you are now evaluating whether this beer is worth one of my 40 vouchers. Alcohol consumption is no longer routine but special and rare. I realize this sounds very controlled and specific, but within months, this process becomes second nature, like riding a bicycle.

A metric will be used to assess if this is a good opportunity or day to consume. Matters that need to be considered are:

1. Who are you drinking with?
2. What kind of alcohol are you planning on drinking and does this alcohol work with the environment you are in?
3. What day of the week and time of day are you drinking?

4. What are your responsibilities while drinking and the next day?
5. Are you celebrating an important milestone?
6. How many times have you drunk this week?
7. Are you in a safe environment?
8. How many drinks do you plan on having?
9. Does having alcohol at this moment add value to this experience?

Here are some of my responses to these questions:

1. Who are you drinking with? I have made it a focus to drink with friends with whom I am comfortable, who have proven to me they can handle alcohol well and do not have any vicious habits, including drug use or negativity while drinking. I really try to avoid drinking around my family, however, I do sometimes and will continue to do so in a reasonable manner as I feel it is important for a person in my demographic, a father of three, to role model how to drink responsibly.
2. What kind of alcohol are you planning on drinking and does this alcohol work with the environment you are in? I think everyone's code for this is different. I believe bourbon, my favorite liquor, is best to be enjoyed in small, comfortable environments. Bourbon leaves me relaxed and still. Almost a numbness. I made a point of having bourbon when visiting with 1-2 friends or at a

dinner event in a small group. I would not consume bourbon at a large party or social event due to the above-mentioned reasons.

3. What day of the week and time of day are you drinking? This question has helped me filter out certain drinking opportunities and stay more centered. I rarely now drink on weekdays and, unless on holidays, never during the day. The thought of having alcohol disrupts and adds friction to the rest of my daily goals and tasks has made cravings at this time go completely extinct.

4. What are your responsibilities while drinking and the next day? Do you have to work, go out in the community, make an important decision or be active with your family? This may be the most important step. Alcohol leads us all to not fire at 100% on physical, mental, psychological and emotional levels. Can you afford to drink and have your commitments the following day be affected by alcohol? If so, you may want to pass on the drinks.

5. Are you celebrating an important milestone or occasion? For me, a few examples of these would be holidays on a beach (preferably without kids) somewhere hot, watching some playoff NFL games, my birthday, a travel location like Las Vegas or Nashville, and occasions where I choose to drink alcohol. Adding reasonable amounts of alcohol to these environments can add value and enjoyment for me.

6. How many times have you drunk this week? I start to get concerned if I go more than two days in a row or three times a week. I understand some weeks will have opportunities for more alcohol, such as an all-inclusive holiday. Be aware of this and try to keep alcohol to once or twice a week on the week you have consumed. Try to string together many multi-week streaks without alcohol throughout the year. I am committed to doing a minimum 40-day dry spell each year moving forward. I highly recommend a cut-and-dry zero booze streak every year, maybe even multiples.

7. Are you in a safe environment? Environmental awareness is important in all facets of life, not just when we choose to consume alcohol. Is there a plan to get home safely? Could you stay over at your friend's house if needed? Are you familiar and trust the people you are with? These are the questions I ask myself before making the drinking choice.

8. How many drinks do you plan on having? Set a mini target for these days. For example, this could include having dinner with friends being an opportunity for 1-2 drinks while a fishing trip up north with no parental or work responsibilities could equate to 4+. Try to stay within your target.

9. Does having alcohol at this moment add value to this experience? This point becomes easier and more second nature after a few months. There are countless examples,

so I just keep asking myself the question and only drink when I feel value is added. Being honest, more than half the time, upon reflecting if value was actually added to the experience, I concluded it was not, so when this happens, take the loss, and brush yourself off and move on. There won't be a perfect time for alcohol every time, just times that end up being better than others.

Chapter 17: PPF-PNN Scale (Past-Present-Future/Positive-Neutral-Negative)

I have created a scale to help with decision-making when choosing to drink or not. I want the individual to consider the past, present, and future when making this choice. Here are some examples:

- **Past**: Has this opportunity led to negative, neutral, or positive outcomes in past experiences?
- **Present**: Could this opportunity have a positive, neutral, or negative outcome?
- **Future:** How will this opportunity affect my next day, considering my physical ability, decision-making, and functioning?

Negative-Neutral-Positive Categories of the PPF Scale

Each opportunity will fall into one of these categories:
- Negative- A decision, action or situation will likely result in a negative experience. This could include anger,

discouragement, frustration, cruel treatment, awkwardness, reputation damage, social or family conflict, or injury.

- Neutral-Negative: A decision, action or situation is likely to be neutral at best but has an opportunity to be negative. Example: Going to a bar, planning on being DD, then drinking and needing to find a ride home.

- Neutral- Decision, action or situation is likely to be neutral. This includes familiarity, comfort, and routine. Example: Have some beers with an old friend in the same environment you have many times before.

- Neutral Positive- A decision, action or situation is likely to be neutral with potential for positivity. Example: This could include attending an event that adds progress, surprise, wisdom, and education, such as a wine tour or whisky tasting with people you are building a friendship or work relationship with or experiencing alcohol while traveling in a new part of the world.

- Positive- A decision, action or situation is likely to be positive. This could include humor, acceptance, happiness, laughter, fun, love and kindness. These feelings are usually based on your favorite people and places you attend, having many safe and memorable experiences. Some examples could be going on a yearly all-inclusive holiday with your wife, friends, or family to a beautiful beach, knowing you have very little personal responsibility and can enjoy alcohol with little risk or consequences. For me, Nashville is my most positive and special place to enjoy alcohol.

You can use this scale to evaluate if certain opportunities are going to be worth the cost of admission. We make thousands of decisions in a day, and I don't want this process to become overwhelming, so let's keep it simple for now. Use this metric when deciding when you want to drink, who you are going to drink with, where you are going to drink, how much you are going to drink, why you are drinking, and what you are going to drink. Here is a quick example:

My best friend Dave Yallup is having a birthday party to celebrate his 40th birthday this coming Saturday. He is inviting ten people over for a BBQ and beer. I like all the people who are going, and the weather is looking to be beautiful. The plan is to arrive after 5 PM. I plan on having a great dinner and drinking 6-8 beers, then take a taxi home.

This sort of quick evaluation will hit subtle targets in your mind and will help pass on certain opportunities to not only not drink but limit putting yourself in a position that has a high likelihood of being negative. We don't need that sort of experience; life is too short to waste in the negative.

Feel free and encouraged to use this PPF-PNN scale for other aspects of life. This could include spending/budgeting, work, recreational choices, and more. I believe this tool is helpful in many facets of decision-making. Evaluating decisions and making informed choices is an art that anyone can attempt to master and help improve their life. The more you reflect and put thought into your decision-making, the more control you have over your life. Using this scale is the equivalent of your brain doing pushups and bicep curls. Always exercise the muscles between your ears!

Chapter 18: More Free 40 Mindset Strategies

Lean on the Metric

When you have a craving, review your metric or criteria for drinking. After a few moments, your mind should shift to refraining due to aspects of your customized indulge mode not being in play. This includes the aforementioned points, such as having to work the following day and having parental or community responsibilities. This process has created a new neuropathway for decision-making regarding alcohol and keeps you more accountable for your relationship with booze. You will drink less because of your new way of thinking. Think of this process as getting your brain ready to train for a marathon and the daily work you have been putting in for months at the mental gym, which has gotten you not only able to complete the race but win it!

Remember, Free 40 does not believe alcohol is inherently bad, just that it should be consumed in a limited manner, with certain boundaries and preparation.

Preparation and asking questions about how an individual can improve any goal, not just their alcohol consumption, is vital in becoming the best versions of ourselves. I believe much of the self-control credited to preparation will have positive effects on other aspects of people's lives. Keep preparing, evaluating, and adjusting, not just with your relationship with alcohol but all parts of your life. Not being hungover and drinking less will make any other goal you have easier to accomplish.

Free Forty is a New Way of Life, Not a Cleanse, Fad or Diet

You probably had the misconception you could keep up the current lifestyle of eating poorly, having irregular sleep, a high drinking frequency, lack of exercise and still get by. Of course, you can. You are a resilient human being who has developed elite coping and adjustment skills. The goal is to believe and execute on the notion of being better and best. Be the best version of yourself. You cannot be the best version of yourself if these factors are lacking or completed in a mediocre way. You cannot be the best version of yourself if you are drinking all the time. This is impossible to achieve.

Mediocrity is outlawed in the Free 40 program. That is not to say mediocrity and failure will never happen in your life. Of course, it will, and these moments are used as ammunition to improve. As Rocky Balboa so eloquently put it, life ain't how hard you hit, it's about how hard you can get hit and keep moving forward. That's how winning is done."

The Value Added

Asking oneself, "Does alcohol add value to this moment?" has been the most helpful thought in curving my drinking. Beers after a sporting event can seem like a rite of passage. Alcohol during Monday night and Thursday night football sounded very reasonable to me for many years. Not anymore. These two examples both take away value when we drink. For golf, drinking after most rounds ends up costing more money, keeps you away from home longer, and opens the door to all the next day's sleep and physical, emotional, and productivity problems that alcohol can bring. The same can be said about drinking during the football games. Both of these games are on weeknights and almost always result in less than average sleep and overconsuming food and alcohol.

Whether I was by myself or watching the game with a few friends, there is no way I could justify alcohol making this experience any better, and the financial, physical, and sleep burden it takes does not add value. Value was being robbed from me. These are just two examples of applying a value-added metric to a given scenario. When you begin doing this every time alcohol is an option, more often than not, drinking will be declined and a new, healthier habit and threshold for alcohol is created. Neuroplasticity changes are in full play with the value-added thought process. Ask yourself regularly, in what environments does alcohol not add value? This mind shift will help you drink less.

Keeping Promises to Yourself

Keeping promises to yourself is important for personal growth and self-discipline. It helps build trust and confidence in yourself and strengthens your character. Making and keeping promises requires commitment and perseverance, especially when faced with challenges or moments of weakness.

The main premise of this book is dedicated to alcohol moderation. It may be difficult at times, but staying true to your promise for one year to have 40 alcohol-free days and then maintaining 40 total alcohol-consumed days throughout the remainder of the year can have numerous benefits for your body, mind, and soul.

In moments of temptation or weakness, remind yourself of the promise you made and why it is important to you. Remember that sticking to your commitment will result in a greater sense of accomplishment and improve your physical and mental well-being.

By successfully keeping your promise, you establish yourself as someone who follows through on what they say. This strengthens your character and builds inner resilience. Each time you overcome a challenge and remain committed, you will feel a sense of fulfillment and pride.

So, when tempted to give up on your promise, don't wave the white flag and quit. Instead, pivot back to your commitment, remembering the benefits it will bring to your life. Stay determined, hold the course, and keep the promises you make to yourself. Your body, mind, and soul will thank you, and you'll continue to grow into a person of integrity and discipline.

Be Compelled to Look to a Higher Power

People vary in their spirituality and belief systems. My suggestion is to lean in and ask for support from any greater power you believe in. Having a conversation with your god, the universe or higher power will assist you in completing Free 40 and living a better life rooted in health, wellness and happiness.

Chapter 19: Finale Aka Cured

I feel cured. Is cured the right word? Possibly, if not, the amount of control I now have over my new relationship with alcohol and how contained my decisions to drink have never been better. This new lifestyle and routine enhanced my life. I feel like I am truly living again. There is nothing I would like more than to help change your life and educate you on the tools that gave me success. I truly hope this book helps you become a better version of yourself. Free 40 is meant for you to lean on, re-read, and use as much as possible. The book is your ally for success.

This is ongoing self-treatment, the same as alcoholics still attending AA meetings. Daily accountability and focus will be needed to hold the course and be alcohol-free for so much of the year. What I have noticed is that this focus and accountability have become second nature. I don't crave drinks. I can say no easily. My energy levels and mood remain optimal and are improving. I am winning every day.

These daily habits and plans being executed have resulted in a new me. The best version of myself.

Will I complete Free 40 forever? That is to be determined. As someone who wants to live beyond 110, I can't imagine drinking up to 300 days like in 2020 and possibly reaching that goal. At this point, I am committed to only drinking 40 days a year, but it is possible that number could go up in time. I can't say to what number, but I don't see myself averaging drinking weekly or greater ever again. That heavy consumption and unaccountable drinking is extinct forever.

Good Fortune and Gratitude

Thank you so much for taking the time to read and review my book and program. I wish you good fortune and encouragement should you decide to go down this path of awareness, accountability, and change. I know you can do this. I believe in you. And I know you are strong enough to make your life better than it has been before. This 365-day investment in your life could be one of the best decisions you have ever made. Let's do Free 40 together.

There is no time like the present to begin this journey to a more fulfilling life.

Tracking Sheet Suggestions

Here are the questions I used as a template during my 40 days of consecutively not drinking and on the 40 days throughout the 365 days, I elected to consume alcohol. Please use these on your phone, computer, or paper, or customize them with the important questions and details you would like to track.

Refrain Mode Questions Day 1-40:

    How were your happiness and energy levels today?

    Did you crave alcohol?

    How would you rate your productivity out of 10?

    Other Observations

Indulge Mode Day 1-40:

    Day of the Week/Date:

    Location:

    Who did you drink with?

    How many drinks did you consume?

What do you feel contributed to your choosing to drink this day?

Did your hangover affect any personal or professional responsibilities the next day?

Rate your overall drinking experience from 1 to 10.

Stay Connected with Aaron Blake

As an author deeply invested in fostering a strong connection with my readers, I am dedicated to providing ongoing support and guidance beyond the pages of my book. I am thrilled to announce the exciting opportunities available to those who wish to embark on a transformative journey towards alcohol moderation and enhanced life skills.

To ensure personalized attention and effective guidance, I am accepting a limited number of clients for alcohol moderation and life coaching services. If you are seeking to improve and rejuvenate your relationship with alcohol or require assistance in navigating life's challenges, I invite you to visit my website at www.free40now.com. There, you will find comprehensive information on the services I offer, along with the option to get in touch and discuss your individual needs.

In addition to one-on-one coaching, I am also enthusiastic about engaging with audiences on a broader scale. I am readily available for public speaking engagements in various settings, including workplaces, institutions, and colleges/universities. Whether it be an inspiring keynote speech or an interactive workshop, my goal is to share my transformative plan and empowering message with as many individuals as possible. I firmly believe that my program can be invaluable in cultivating personal growth, resilience, healthy habits and a much-improved relationship with alcohol.

Wherever my plan and message can be of assistance, I am eager to make a positive impact. By embracing opportunities for collaboration, I aim to create a platform for individuals to connect, learn, and overcome obstacles together.

Stay connected with me as we embark on this journey toward personal and collective transformation.

Visit www.free40now.com to explore the multitude of ways we can work together. Let us seize every opportunity to unlock our potential, foster meaningful connections, and inspire positive change.

Website www.free40now.com

Acknowledgements

There are many people I would like to thank for helping motivate me to write this book and design Free 40. These include, but are not limited to, my wife Vanessa and sons Jagger, River, and Maverick. Some major social media influencers who inspired me along the way are:

Pamela Reif: For teaching me how to relax my mind and become more health conscious, aware, and flexible. I could not sit cross-legged until I watched your YouTube videos.

Odette Cressler: For your passion, honesty, vulnerability, and dedication to alcohol recovery and unparalleled awareness of how alcohol can affect one's self. Odette is one of the most aware individuals I have listened to.

Ed Mylett: For the constant motivation on so many different levels of life, including health, mindset, work and family, and the best reminder that all of us were put on Earth to do something great.

Jason Selk: For constantly teaching one's self to lean into a solution and pose the question of what's the one thing I can do right now to improve?

About the Author

Aaron Blake is not just another author advocating for alcohol moderation and awareness; he is a testament to the transformative power of self-realization and determination. A married father to three loving children, Aaron deeply reflected on his relationship with alcohol and embarked on a personal journey that led him to design a program that would revolutionize his relationship with alcohol and, subsequently, his entire life.

In his groundbreaking book, titled "Free 40," Aaron shares his riveting tale of personal triumph, with the ultimate goal of bestowing happiness, health, and boundless energy upon every individual who partakes in this method of alcohol moderation. His words unlock the door to a realm of enlightenment rarely witnessed before, inviting readers to shatter the chains that bind them to their self-destructive habits while helping create the best version of themselves.

Blake's program is as meticulous as it is magnificent. With an unwavering commitment to fostering well-being, he presents a holistic approach that suggests the reader reevaluate their personal alcohol habits. By adding humorous anecdotes and practical motivating concepts, he presents a new way of looking at different approaches to reducing alcohol consumption. Bursting with earnestness and anchored in personal experience, Free 40 offers a roadmap to lasting change.

Aaron Blake's resolute dedication to helping others change their relationship with alcohol shines through the pages of this awe-inspiring book. Spare not a moment to uncover the secrets that transformed his life into a beacon of hope and inspiration, illuminating the path towards a brighter, alcohol-reduced future.

Manufactured by Amazon.ca
Bolton, ON